THE HOUND OF BASKERVILLES

by
Sir Arthur Conan Doyle

Student Packet

Written by
Joan F. Langham

Contains masters for: 2 Prereading Activities
5 Vocabulary Activities
1 Study Guide
4 Character Analysis Activities
4 Literary Analysis Activities
2 Comprehension Activities
2 Critical Thinking Activities
1 Writing Activity
5 Quizzes
1 Novel Test

PLUS   Detailed Answer Key
and Scoring Rubric

Note

The Signet Classic paperback version of the novel, © 2001, was used to prepare this guide. Page references may differ in other editions. Novel ISBN: 0-451-52801-8

Please note: Please assess the appropriateness of this book for the age level and maturity of your students prior to reading and discussing it with them.

ISBN 1-58130-856-6

Copyright infringement is a violation of Federal Law.

© 2005 by Novel Units, Inc., Bulverde, Texas. All rights reserved. No part of this publication may be reproduced, stored in a retrieval system, or transmitted in any way or by any means electronic, mechanical, photocopying, recording, or otherwise) without prior written permission from Novel Units, Inc.

Photocopying of student worksheets by a classroom teacher at a non-profit school who has purchased this publication for his/her own class is permissible. Reproduction of any part of this publication for an entire school or for a school system, by for-profit institutions and tutoring centers, or for commercial sale is strictly prohibited.

Novel Units is a registered trademark of Novel Units, Inc. Printed in the United States of America.

To order, contact your local school supply store, or—
Novel Units, Inc.
P.O. Box 97
Bulverde, TX 78163-0097

Web site: www.educyberstor.com

Lori Mammen, Editorial Director
Andrea M. Harris, Production Manager/Production Specialist
Suzanne K. Mammen, Curriculum Specialist
Heather Johnson, Product Development Specialist
Vicky Rainwater, Curriculum Specialist
Jill Reed, Product Development Specialist
Nancy Smith, Product Development Specialist
Adrienne Speer, Production Specialist
Lenella Meister, Production Specialist

Name _____

The Hound of the Baskervilles
Activity #1 • Prereading
Use Before Reading

Be a Detective!

Directions: Check out the book by looking at the cover and thumbing through the pages. Then, ask yourself who, what, where, when, why, and how. Write your questions in the spaces below. Exchange papers with a partner and answer each other's questions.

Who?

What?

Where?

When?

Why?

How?

Name _____

The Hound of the Baskervilles
Activity #2 • Prereading
Use Before Reading

Directions: Read the terms below and consider their importance to the novel. Freewrite for at least three minutes on the possible significance of each and predict what the novel will be about.

1. legend

2. hound

3. family curse

4. detective

5. the moors

6. mystery

7. inheritance

8. warnings

9. murder

10. terror

Name _____

The Hound of the Baskervilles
Activity #3 • Vocabulary
Chapters 1–3, pp. 9–45

Vocabulary Chart

ferrule (10)	erroneous (11)	incredulously (13)	astutely (14)
anthropological (16)	wanton (21)	leagues (22)	anon (23)
bemused (23)	*roysterers (24)	scion (26)	prosaic (28)
chimerical (31)	diabolical (37)	immaculate (41)	

*archaic spelling

Directions: Write each vocabulary word in the left-hand column of the chart. Complete the chart by placing a check mark in the column that best describes your familiarity with each word. Working with a partner, find and read the line where each word appears in the story. Find the meaning of each word in the dictionary. Together with your partner, choose ten of the words checked in the last column. On a separate sheet of paper, use each of those words in a sentence.

Vocabulary Word	I Can Define	I Have Seen/Heard	New Word For Me

Name _____

The Hound of the Baskervilles
Activity #4 • Vocabulary
Chapters 4–6, pp. 46–91

Vocabulary Sentence Sets

pugnacious (46)	foolscap (47)	bourgeois (50)	singular (53)
languid (57)	hansom (58)	malevolent (59)	articulate (65)
entailed (69)	inexplicable (72)	toff (76)	imprudent (80)
bracken (83)	equestrian (83)	atrocious (84)	surmounted (85)
crenellated (86)	mullioned (86)	balustraded (89)	resonant (90)

Directions: Choose 15 vocabulary words from the list above. Write the words on the numbered lines below.

1. _____   2. _____
3. _____   4. _____
5. _____   6. _____
7. _____   8. _____
9. _____   10. _____
11. _____   12. _____
13. _____   14. _____
15. _____

On a separate sheet of paper, use each of the following sets of words in an original sentence. Your sentences should show that you know the meanings of the vocabulary words as they are used in the story.

Sentence 1: words 8 and 4
Sentence 2: words 9 and 3
Sentence 3: words 1 and 10
Sentence 4: words 11 and 7
Sentence 5: words 15 and 13
Sentence 6: words 3 and 6
Sentence 7: words 12 and 4
Sentence 8: words 14 and 9
Sentence 9: words 5 and 2
Sentence 10: words 7 and 6

Name _____

The Hound of the Baskervilles
Activity #5 • Vocabulary
Chapters 7–9, pp. 92–144

Crossword Puzzle

Across
2. massive stones
4. easily angered; hot-tempered
6. not readily understood; mysterious
7. trick; plan intended to mislead
11. disapproval
14. publicly scorned
15. expressive of urgency or command
17. unchanging; absolute; definite
18. troublesome
19. one who studies ancient people or times

Down
1. unconcerned
3. aged; wrinkled
5. shifty; sly
8. moving in a flowing or wavelike manner
9. spotty; blotched
10. watchful; cautious
12. secretly; deliberately; slowly
13. advantageous; favorable
16. pale; lacking sparkle or liveliness

Name _____

The Hound of the Baskervilles
Activity #6 • Vocabulary
Chapters 10–12, pp. 145–193

Word Map

sodden (153)	morass (153)	equivocal (155)	almoner (162)
reticent (166)	roughshod (168)	incredulity (170)	solicitations (172)
dilapidated (173)	pannikin (174)	malignant (175)	tenacity (178)
irrevocable (188)	precipitous (188)	paroxysm (189)	

Directions: Choose at least three words from the vocabulary list above. Complete the word map below for each of your words.

Synonyms

Magazine cut-out, drawing, or symbol that shows what the word means

Word

Definition in your own words

Word used in a sentence

Name _____

The Hound of the Baskervilles
Activity #7 • Vocabulary
Chapters 13–15, pp. 194–240

Vocabulary Chart

connoisseur (199)	implicitly (202)	serrated (214)	exultant (216)
hackles (216)	mastiff (217)	doddering (219)	swathed (220)
dupe (221)	quagmires (222)	miasmatic (222)	barrister (227)
purloined (228)	finesse (230)	specious (231)	expedient (233)
audacity (233)	elucidate (234)		

Directions: Complete the chart using the vocabulary words above.

Noun	Verb	Adjective	Adverb

Bonus: Now that you have completed the chart, use the vocabulary words to write a mystery story of your own.

Name _____

The Hound of the Baskervilles
Study Guide

Directions: Answer the following questions on a separate sheet of paper. Use your answers in class discussions, for writing assignments, and to review for tests.

Chapters 1–3, pp. 9–45

1. What item has been left at Sherlock Holmes' office? To whom does the item belong?
2. What conclusions does Dr. Watson make about the item?
3. How does Holmes react to Watson's theories?
4. Who arrives at Holmes' home?
5. What is the purpose of Dr. Mortimer's visit?
6. Briefly summarize the contents of the manuscript.
7. What has happened to Sir Charles Baskerville?
8. What bits of information were excluded from Sir Charles' obituary?
9. Who is scheduled to arrive in London?
10. Why isn't Holmes concerned about Sir Henry going to Baskerville Hall?
11. What important deduction does Holmes make about Sir Charles?

Chapters 4–6, pp. 46–91

1. What does Sir Henry receive upon his arrival in London?
2. What does Holmes conclude about the note?
3. How does Sir Henry feel about the note and the subsequent disappearance of his boots?
4. What does Holmes suggest Sir Henry do? How does Sir Henry respond?
5. What do Holmes and Watson discover after Sir Henry and Dr. Mortimer leave?
6. What is Cartwright's assignment?
7. Who does Sir Henry think might be the man following them around London?
8. How does Holmes plan to determine if Barrymore is actually the man following them?
9. Why does Holmes send Dr. Watson to Baskerville Hall instead of going there himself?
10. What does Holmes learn from the cabman?
11. What frightening news awaits Sir Henry, Dr. Mortimer, and Watson when they arrive in Devonshire?
12. Who greets the travelers at Baskerville Hall? What do they tell Sir Henry?
13. What does Watson hear late at night at Baskerville Hall?

Name _____

The Hound of the Baskervilles
Study Guide
page 2

Chapters 7–9, pp. 92–144

1. How does Watson know that Barrymore is lying about his wife crying at night?
2. Why wasn't Holmes' plan to discover the whereabouts of Barrymore successful?
3. Whom does Watson meet on the moor? What does he tell Watson about the moors?
4. What does Stapleton say that startles Watson? How does Stapleton rationalize having this information?
5. How does Stapleton describe the Grimpen Mire? What extraordinary claim does he make regarding the Mire?
6. Who approaches Watson while Stapleton is chasing the butterfly? What does she tell Watson? Why does she tell him this?
7. Briefly summarize Watson's first report to Holmes.
8. Briefly summarize Watson's second report to Holmes.
9. How does Watson feel about his assignment to observe the events at Baskerville Hall?

Chapters 10–12, pp. 145–193

1. Why is Watson feeling increasingly ill at ease?
2. Why is Barrymore upset with Sir Henry?
3. What does Barrymore tell Sir Henry in return for his promise not to reveal Selden's whereabouts to the police? Why had he kept this information a secret?
4. What does Watson discover about the woman Sir Charles was waiting for on the night of his death?
5. What does Barrymore reveal about the dark stranger on the moor?
6. What is Watson's first impression upon meeting Laura Lyons?
7. Why did Ms. Lyons write Sir Charles the letter asking to meet with him?
8. What useful information does Frankland unknowingly give to Watson?
9. Who is the dark stranger on the moor?
10. Why has Holmes been concealing his identity?
11. What does Holmes reveal to Watson about the Stapletons and Laura Lyons?
12. What conclusion has Holmes come to regarding the threats on Sir Henry?
13. What has happened to Selden? Why?
14. Who arrives on the moor as Watson and Holmes are inspecting the body? How does he react upon seeing Selden's body?

Name _____

The Hound of the Baskervilles
Study Guide
page 3

Chapters 13–15, pp. 194–240

1. What does Holmes deduce after looking at the portraits in Baskerville Hall?
2. What does Holmes tell Sir Henry the next morning? What does he instruct Sir Henry to do?
3. Whose help does Holmes enlist in preparation for apprehending Stapleton?
4. Why do Holmes and Watson visit Laura Lyons?
5. What does Ms. Lyons tell Holmes regarding Stapleton and her meeting with Sir Charles?
6. What do Holmes, Watson, and Lestrade observe upon sneaking to Stapleton's house?
7. What happens when Sir Henry leaves Stapleton's house?
8. Briefly describe the Hound of the Baskervilles.
9. What caused the hound's frightening appearance?
10. Whom do Holmes, Watson, and Lestrade find tied up in Stapleton's house? What does she tell the three men?
11. What do Holmes and Watson find in the Mire? What was it used for?
12. What happens to Stapleton?
13. What do Holmes and Watson discover about Stapleton's identity?
14. What were Stapleton's motives for his crimes against the Baskervilles? How was he so easily able to commit these crimes?

Name _____

The Hound of the Baskervilles
Activity #8 • Character Analysis
Use During Reading

Sociogram

Directions: On the "spokes" surrounding each character's name, write several adjectives that describe that character. How does one character influence the other? On the arrows joining one character to another, write a description of the relationship between the two characters. Remember, relationships go both ways, so each line requires a descriptive word.

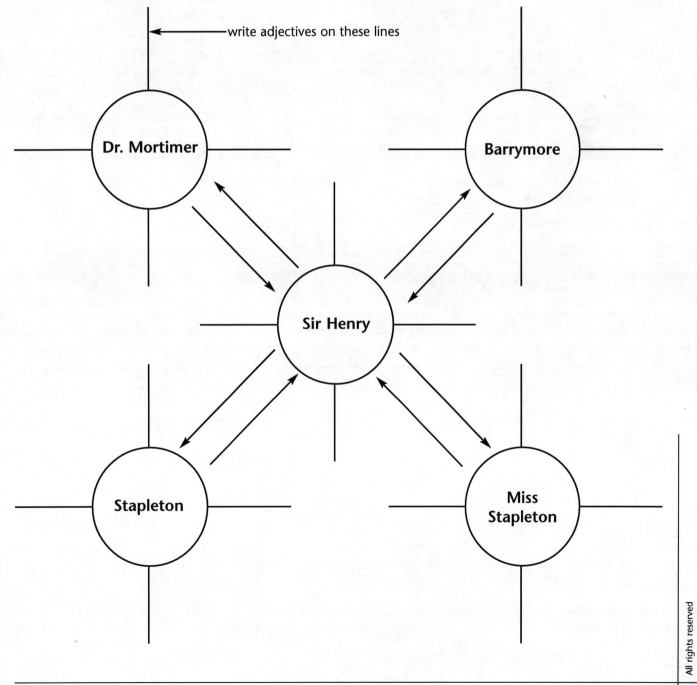

© Novel Units, Inc. 13

Name _____

The Hound of the Baskervilles
Activity #9 • Literary Analysis
Use During Reading

Story Map

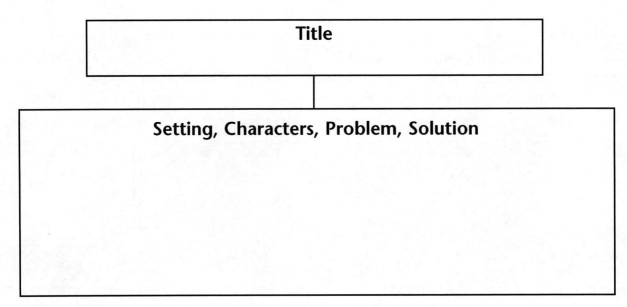

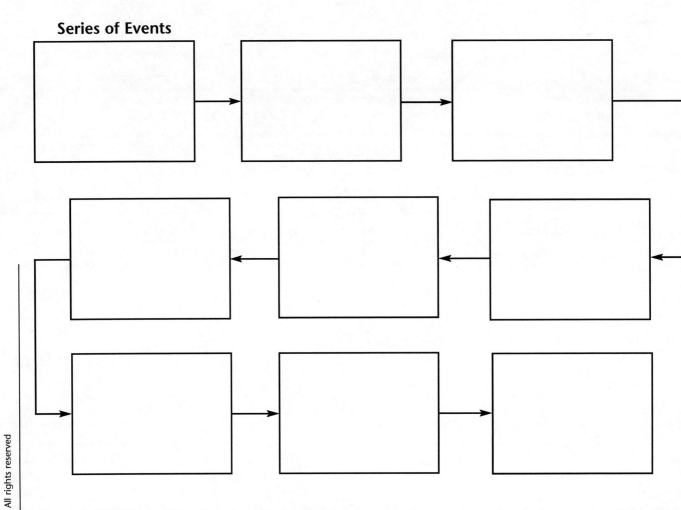

Name _____

The Hound of the Baskervilles
Activity #10 • Literary Analysis
Use During Reading

Clue Log

Directions: When you read something you think might be important later in the novel, write it down. See if you can solve the book's mystery.

Page	Clue (event or item)	Could have something to do with—

Name _____

The Hound of the Baskervilles
Activity #11 • Character Analysis
Use During/After Reading

Character Analysis Blocks

Directions: Select a character from the book to describe using the blocks below.

Who is the character?

What does the character do?	Why does s/he do it?

What, if anything, is significant about the character's name?	What is the nature of this character's actions? (reactive, active, important, consequential, secondary)	What is the significance of the book's time and place to the character?

What is unusual or important about the character?	How does the character change in the story?	Does the character remind you of another character from another book? Who?	Do you know anyone similar to this character?

16 | © Novel Units, Inc.

Name _____

The Hound of the Baskervilles
Activity #12 • Comprehension
Use During/After Reading

Inference Flow Chart

Directions: Fill in the boxes of the flow chart with the events portrayed in the story. In the ovals beneath, state what emotions and feelings are inferred. The chart has been started for you.

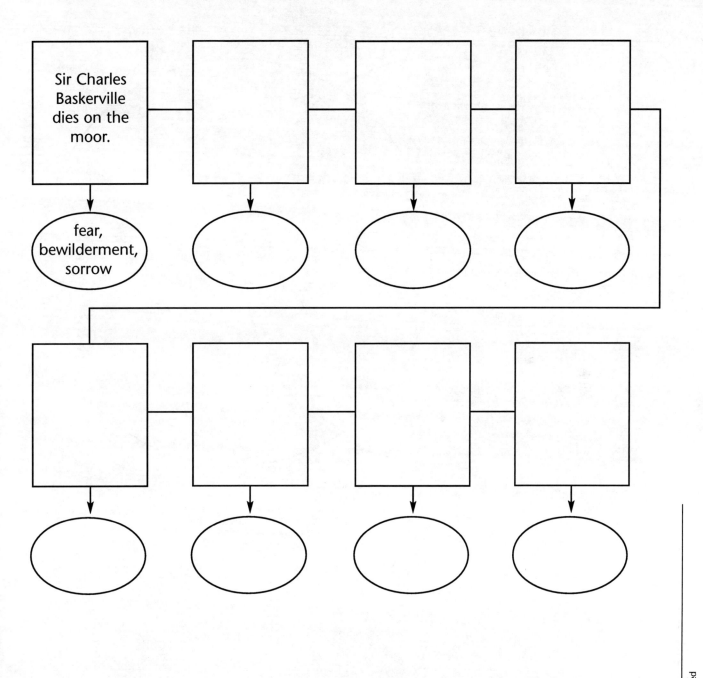

Name _____

The Hound of the Baskervilles
Activity #13 • Comprehension
Use During/After Reading

Venn Diagram

Directions: Compare and contrast Sir Charles and Sir Henry Baskerville.

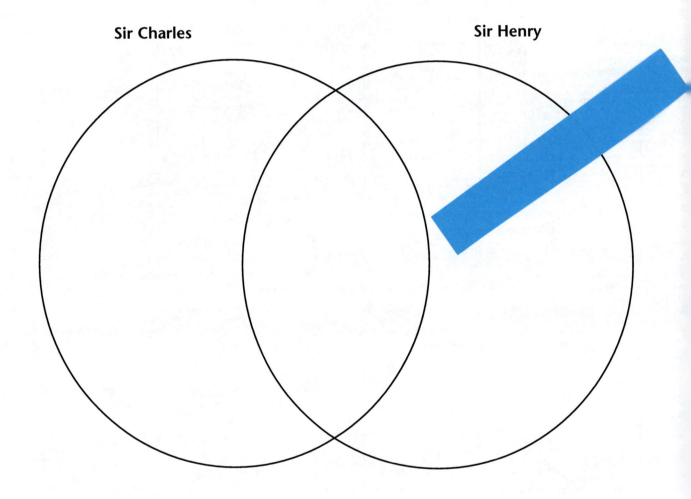

Name _____

The Hound of the Baskervilles
Activity #14 • Literary Analysis
Use During/After Reading

Graphing Plot Lines

Climax

Resolution

Building Action

Beginning

Characters

Setting

Problem

Name _____

The Hound of the Baskervilles
Activity #15 • Critical Thinking
Use After Reading

Using Dialogue

Directions: Choose some dialogue from the book. Fill in the chart to evaluate the purpose of the dialogue and whether or not it is effective in moving along the plot.

- Extra Credit—extra bits of dialogue I remember from my outside reading
- Who is speaking?
- How is the plot advanced with these words?
- What is special about the dialogue?
- What does the dialogue tell me about the characters speaking?

Dialogue on Pages _____

Name _____

The Hound of the Baskervilles
Activity #16 • Critical Thinking
Use After Reading

Recognizing Red Herrings

Directions: A red herring is a person or event that distracts you from the real solution to a problem or mystery. Write the name of a person or list a circumstance in each box that could qualify as a red herring in *The Hound of the Baskervilles*.

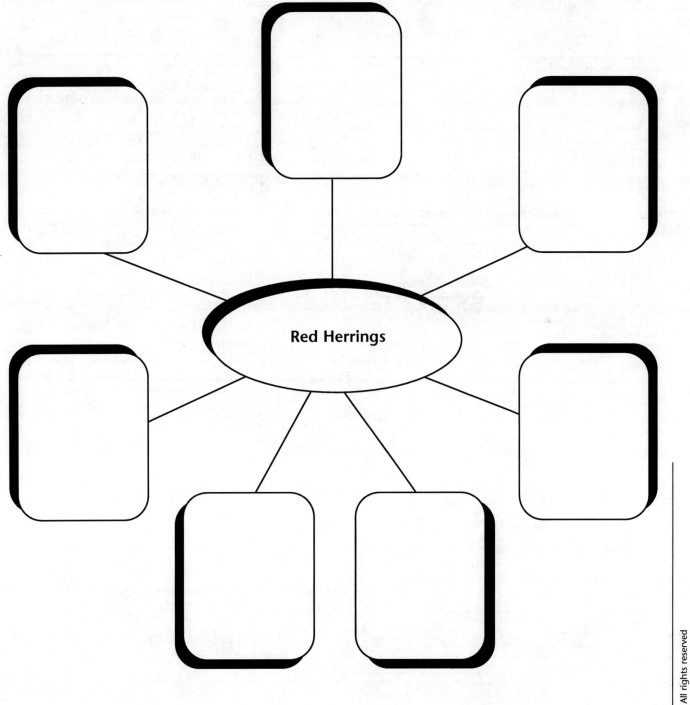

Name _____

The Hound of the Baskervilles
Activity #17 • Character Analysis
Use After Reading

Feelings

Directions: Choose a character from the book and complete the chart below.

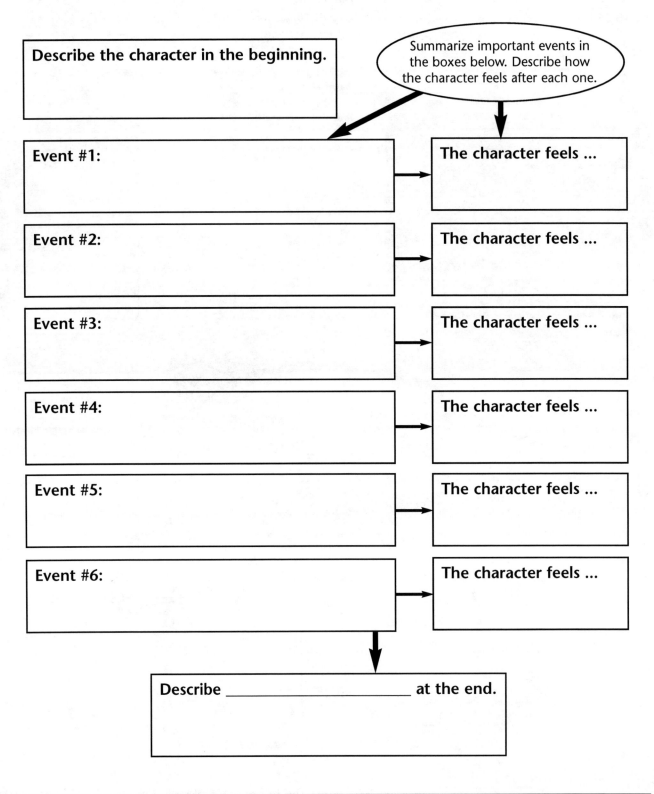

Name _____

The Hound of the Baskervilles
Activity #18 • Character Analysis
Use After Reading

Character Attribute Chart

Directions: Complete the chart below. After completing the chart, choose one of the persons you listed in the last column and write a brief biography about him/her.

Character	One-word Description	Appearance	Significance to the Story	Do you know anyone similar?
Sherlock Holmes				
Dr. Watson				
Sir Henry				
Stapleton				
Miss Stapleton				

Name _____

The Hound of the Baskervilles
Activity #19 • Literary Analysis
Use After Reading

Cause/Effect Map

Directions: List the causes of Sir Charles Baskerville's death in the boxes below.

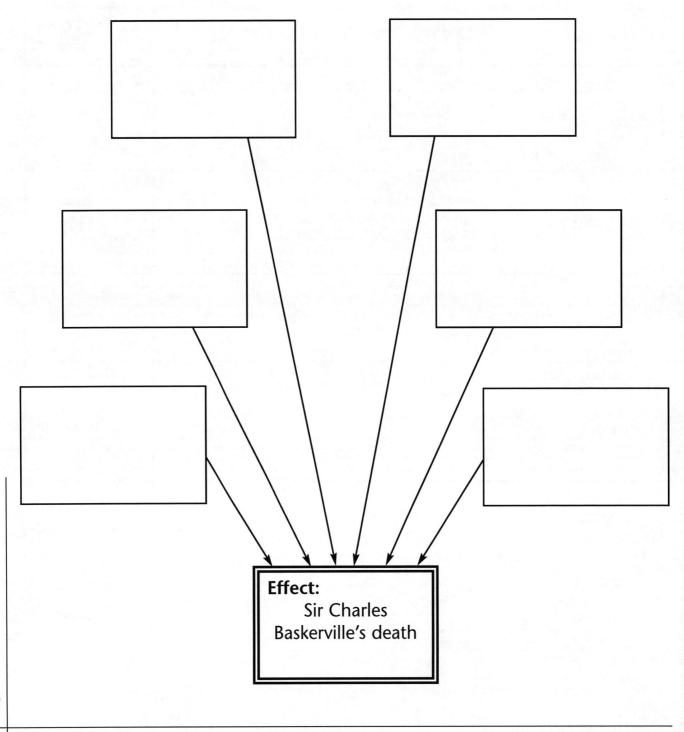

Name _____

The Hound of the Baskervilles
Activity #20 • Writing
Use After Reading

Editorial

Directions: Write a newspaper article about Stapleton's death. Include information about his crimes and his mysterious disappearance while being pursued across the moor.

Devonshire Daily

Name _____

The Hound of the Baskervilles
Quiz #1
Chapters 1–3, pp. 9–45

Identification

Directions: Match the items in Column A with the correct description in Column B.

Column A

_____ 1. Sir Henry Baskerville

_____ 2. Sherlock Holmes

_____ 3. Dr. Mortimer

_____ 4. manuscript

_____ 5. Dr. Watson

_____ 6. John Barrymore

_____ 7. the Hound of the Baskervilles

_____ 8. Sir Charles Baskerville

_____ 9. moors

_____ 10. Hugo Baskerville

Column B

a. intrigues Holmes to take the case

b. legendary curse on Baskerville family

c. mysterious setting for most of novel

d. trusted colleague of Sherlock Holmes

e. heir to Baskerville estate

f. arrogant London detective

g. horrible man; reason for family curse

h. Baskerville family physician

i. house servant at Baskerville Hall

j. victim of the beastly hound

Name _____

The Hound of the Baskervilles
Quiz #2
Chapters 4–6, pp. 46–91

A. True/False

___ 1. Sir Charles Baskerville receives a note warning him to stay away from the moors.

___ 2. Stapleton is the man initially suspected of following Sir Henry in London.

___ 3. Sherlock Holmes sends a telegram to Baskerville Hall.

___ 4. The cabman in London had a passenger who claimed to be Dr. Watson.

___ 5. A convict is hiding in the Devonshire moors.

___ 6. Watson hears a woman sobbing late at night at Baskerville Hall.

B. Short Answer

7. How does Sir Henry feel about the threats being made against him?

8. What does Holmes instruct Cartwright to do?

9. Why does Holmes send Dr. Watson with Sir Henry to Baskerville Hall?

10. How does Holmes know that the man following Sir Henry in London is clever?

11. What do Mr. and Mrs. Barrymore tell Sir Henry upon his arrival at Baskerville Hall?

12. What is Watson's impression of Baskerville Hall and the surrounding moors?

Name _____

The Hound of the Baskervilles
Quiz #3
Chapters 7–9, pp. 92–144

Fill in the Blanks
Directions: Complete the paragraph below.

Watson and (1)_____ are now at (2)_____. They both have heard a woman crying in the night and believe that it is (3)_____. Watson discovers that the (4)_____ Holmes sent was not given directly to the addressee, so Holmes could not discover if Barrymore was really in Devonshire. While out on the moor, Mr. (5)_____ of Merripit House introduces himself and chats with Watson. He points out the (6)_____, which often swallows up moor ponies that wander into it. The two men hear a mournful (7)_____, and both believe it is the (8)_____. (9)_____ mistakes (10)_____ for (11)_____. Because of the error, she warns him to leave (12)_____ and not to tell (13)_____ that she has made this warning. Watson later reports to (14)_____ that the (15)_____ on the moor has probably gone away and that (16)_____ has become enamored with Miss Stapleton. A strange occurrence at night is also included in Watson's report. He has seen (17)_____ at the window, looking out over the moor and signaling with a (18)_____. Sir Henry and Watson discover that he is signaling to (19)_____, the criminal, who turns out to be the younger (20)_____ of (21)_____. Sir Henry's servants have been helping the criminal by giving him (22)_____. Watson and Sir Henry decide to pursue (23)_____ by going out on the moor at night. While there, they hear the baying of the hound and see a silhouette of a (24)_____ on the moor.

Name _____

The Hound of the Baskervilles
Quiz #4
Chapters 10–12, pp. 145–193

Multiple Choice
Directions: Choose the best answer for each of the following.

____ 1. Barrymore is upset because Sir Henry
    (a) has fired the Barrymores
    (b) is not afraid of the hound
    (c) has been looking for Selden
    (d) is in love with Miss Stapleton

____ 2. Why was Sir Charles on the moor the night of his death?
    (a) Dr. Mortimer asked to see him.
    (b) He was meeting a woman by the gate.
    (c) He was waiting for Sir Henry's arrival.
    (d) Mr. Barrymore suggested he take a walk.

____ 3. Watson discovers that the dark stranger lives
    (a) in a stone hut on the hillside
    (b) near Baskerville Hall
    (c) in a cave dug out on the moors
    (d) with the Stapletons at Merripit House

____ 4. Laura Lyons wished to meet with Sir Charles in order to
    (a) ask questions about Stapleton
    (b) warn him about the hound
    (c) ask him for money
    (d) seduce him

____ 5. Who reveals the most useful information about the dark stranger on the moor?
    (a) Miss Stapleton
    (b) Mr. Frankland
    (c) Dr. Mortimer
    (d) Cartwright

____ 6. Watson discovers that the dark stranger is really Sherlock Holmes when he
    (a) sees Holmes' face
    (b) sees Holmes' cloak
    (c) hears Holmes' voice
    (d) smells Holmes' tobacco

Name _____

The Hound of the Baskervilles
Quiz #4
page 2

_____ 7. Holmes reveals all BUT which of the following to Watson?
(a) the actual identity of Miss Stapleton
(b) Laura Lyons' relationship to Stapleton
(c) the name of the man who followed them in London
(d) the whereabouts of the criminal, Selden

_____ 8. How is Stapleton able to carry out his crimes?
(a) He only comes out of his house at night.
(b) Everyone is afraid of the hound.
(c) He stalks Sir Henry and Dr. Watson.
(d) Everyone is afraid of him.

_____ 9. The hound attacks and kills Selden because he is
(a) running across the moors
(b) chasing the Stapletons
(c) taunting the hound
(d) dressed in Sir Henry's clothes

_____ 10. How does Stapleton react when he sees that Selden is dead?
(a) surprised
(b) upset
(c) happy
(d) unconcerned

Name _____

The Hound of the Baskervilles
Quiz #5
Chapters 13–15, pp. 194–240

Identification
Directions: Match each mystery to its solution.

Mystery

_____ 1. supernatural hound

_____ 2. the cryptic warning

_____ 3. Stapleton's relationship with his sister

_____ 4. the missing boots

_____ 5. Sir Charles waiting at gate

_____ 6. the bearded man in London

_____ 7. L.L.

_____ 8. disappearance of Stapleton

_____ 9. whereabouts of Miss Stapleton

_____10. Mrs. Barrymore crying at night

Solution

a. fell into the Grimpen Mire

b. tied up in house

c. worried about brother, Selden

d. Stapleton

e. Frankland's daughter

f. sent by Miss Stapleton

g. sister is really his wife

h. gave Sir Henry's scent to hound

i. received note from woman

j. phosphorus application

The Hound of the Baskervilles
Name _____
Novel Test

Novel Test
A. Identification

____ 1. Sherlock Holmes
____ 2. Dr. Watson
____ 3. Dr. Mortimer
____ 4. Jack Stapleton
____ 5. Miss Stapleton
____ 6. Mr. Frankland
____ 7. Laura Lyons
____ 8. Sir Charles Baskerville
____ 9. Sir Henry Baskerville
____ 10. John Barrymore
____ 11. Mrs. Barrymore
____ 12. Selden
____ 13. Hugo Baskerville

a. love interest of Sir Henry
b. a naturalist
c. Laura Lyons' father
d. expert detective
e. Stapleton's girlfriend
f. origin of Baskerville curse
g. heir to the Baskerville estate
h. maid at Baskerville Hall
i. butler at Baskerville Hall
j. escaped criminal
k. ailing man chased by hound
l. Baskerville family physician
m. colleague of Sherlock Holmes

B. Multiple Choice

____ 14. What information is missing from Sir Charles' obituary?
 (a) Sir Charles was clutching dog hair.
 (b) A dog's footprint was nearby.
 (c) A dog was seen in the neighborhood.
 (d) He was meeting someone on the moor.

____ 15. How does Dr. Mortimer know that Sir Charles lingers at the end of the yew lane?
 (a) The Barrymores checked the time he went out.
 (b) A neighbor saw him there as he was going to town.
 (c) Sir Charles told Mortimer he was going to linger outside.
 (d) There were ashes scattered about.

The Hound of the Baskervilles
Novel Test
page 2

Name _____

____ 16. Why are Sir Henry's boots stolen?
    (a) to get his scent
    (b) to get his footprint
    (c) to get his shoe size
    (d) to get his favorite style

____ 17. What evidence confirms that there really is a hound upon the moor?
    (a) There are sightings of it.
    (b) A dog kennel is discovered.
    (c) Half-eaten animals are found.
    (d) Someone says they sold a dog to a neighbor.

____ 18. Who receives a cryptic note?
    (a) Sherlock Holmes
    (b) Dr. Watson
    (c) Sir Henry Baskerville
    (d) Sir Charles Baskerville

____ 19. Who is revealed to be the author of the note?
    (a) John Barrymore
    (b) Selden
    (c) Mrs. Barrymore
    (d) Miss Stapleton

____ 20. Why does Holmes send Cartwright to dig through hotel trashcans?
    (a) to find the newspaper that the letters were cut from
    (b) to check the time an event occurred
    (c) to find the stolen black boot
    (d) to find a lost telegram from Stapleton

____ 21. How does Holmes attempt to discern if Barrymore is in Devonshire?
    (a) calls on the telephone
    (b) sends a spy out
    (c) sends a telegraph
    (d) asks the locals

____ 22. What is the name of the dangerous, swampy part of the moor?
    (a) Wuthering Hole
    (b) Devonshire Dip
    (c) English Moor Swamp
    (d) Grimpen Mire

Name _____

The Hound of the Baskervilles
Novel Test
page 3

____ 23. What mistake does Miss Stapleton make when she meets Dr. Watson?
(a) tells her husband a lie
(b) leaves a piece of her clothing in town
(c) thinks Watson is Sir Henry
(d) sends a note to the wrong person

____ 24. How does Barrymore signal out to the moor at night?
(a) reflects light off a mirror
(b) turns lights off and on
(c) uses a candle
(d) rings a bell

____ 25. Who is the dark stranger on the moor?
(a) Dr. Mortimer
(b) Cartwright
(c) Sherlock Holmes
(d) Selden

____ 26. Why did Laura Lyons want to meet with Sir Charles?
(a) She needed advice.
(b) She needed an address of a person.
(c) She needed to tell him a secret about Stapleton.
(d) She needed financial help again.

____ 27. What happens to Selden on the moor?
(a) He runs into Stapleton.
(b) He is killed by the hound.
(c) He is captured by Lestrade.
(d) He falls into the Grimpen Mire.

____ 28. What is Stapleton's motive for wanting Sir Henry Baskerville dead?
(a) an inheritance
(b) jealousy
(c) revenge
(d) mutual love interest

Name _____

The Hound of the Baskervilles
Novel Test
page 4

____ 29. What makes the hound appear supernatural and beastly?
   (a) huge fangs and long legs
   (b) phosphorus
   (c) piercing cry
   (d) speed

____ 30. Which words best describe Stapleton?
   (a) pleasant and kind
   (b) deceiving and brutal
   (c) ignorant and careless
   (d) consistent and carefree

C. True and False

_____ 31. Watson is aware that Holmes is hiding on the moor.

_____ 32. Mrs. Barrymore is often distraught over Selden's plight.

_____ 33. The Stapletons have a strained and unusual relationship.

_____ 34. Sherlock Holmes discovers that Stapleton is a Baskerville.

_____ 35. Stapleton dies when the hound attacks him.

_____ 36. Miss Stapleton tells Holmes where her husband is hiding.

_____ 37. Laura Lyons was aware of Stapleton's plot to kill Sir Charles.

_____ 38. The hound is half-starved and hidden on the moor.

D. Essay: Complete one of the following in a well-developed essay. Cite specific examples from the novel to support your ideas.

1. How does the setting add to the atmosphere and suspense of the story?
2. Discuss what makes Sherlock Holmes a clever and brilliant detective.

Answer Key

Activities #1–#4: Answers will vary.

Activity #5: See completed puzzle on page 39 of this guide.

Activity #6: Answers will vary.

Activity #7: Nouns—connoisseur, hackles, mastiff, dupe, quagmires, barrister, finesse, audacity; Verbs—purloined, elucidate; Adjectives—serrated, exultant, doddering, swathed, miasmatic, specious, expedient; Adverbs—implicitly; Stories will vary.

Study Guide

Chapters 1–3, pp. 9–45: 1. an engraved cane; Dr. James Mortimer (p. 9) 2. He believes that Dr. Mortimer must be a successful and elderly country doctor who walks to see his patients. He also concludes from the engraved inscription that the cane was given to Dr. Mortimer by members of a certain hunting group (p. 10). 3. positively at first, then says that because Watson was completely wrong, he (Sherlock Holmes) is now able to make the correct theories (pp. 10–12) 4. Dr. Mortimer (p. 15) 5. He has brought an old manuscript for Holmes' review (p. 19). 6. It tells of the origin of a family curse, the Hound of the Baskervilles. Long ago, Hugo Baskerville, a rude and horrible man, kidnapped and tried to take advantage of a young girl. When she escaped, Hugo and his friends pursued her across the moor. An enormous hound attacked and killed Hugo, thus beginning the curse. Since then, many Baskervilles have died horrible deaths, giving strength to the legend of the hound (pp. 21–25). 7. On May 4, Sir Charles went on his usual nighttime walk and never returned. His house servant became worried and went looking for him, finding him dead in an alley, apparently having suffered from a heart attack (pp. 26–28). 8. There were footprints of a giant hound on the ground near Sir Charles' body (p. 32). 9. Sir Henry Baskerville, the heir to the Baskerville estate (p. 37) 10. Holmes believes that if, in fact, there is a supernatural curse on the Baskerville family, Sir Henry is not in any more danger at the hall than he is elsewhere (pp. 38–39). 11. Holmes does not believe Sir Charles was tip-toeing through the alley, as Dr. Mortimer implied. Holmes believes the mark of the footprints changed because, just prior to Sir Charles' death, the man was running for his life (pp. 43–44).

Chapters 4–6, pp. 46–91: 1. a note warning him to stay away from the moor (pp. 47–48) 2. It was cut from the *Times* with nail scissors, sent by an educated person wanting to appear uneducated, and prepared hurriedly by someone in a hotel (pp. 50–52). 3. He is very confused by the meaning of the note. He is very angry about the disappearance of his boots. Neither event, however, frightens him as it is intended to do. 4. Holmes says that perhaps Sir Henry should not go to Baskerville Hall. Sir Henry stubbornly refuses to be frightened away from his family's home (p. 56). 5. Someone has been following Sir Henry since he arrived in London (p. 58). 6. Holmes asks him to visit 23 hotels and check the trash for the newspaper used to make the note (p. 61). 7. Sir Charles' house servant and butler, Barrymore (p. 67) 8. He will send a telegram to Baskerville Hall with instructions that it be delivered directly into Barrymore's hands (p. 67). 9. He claims that he is too busy with his other cases to leave London. He ensures Sir Henry and Dr. Mortimer that Watson is a very capable man (p. 70). 10. The man that has been following Sir Henry told the cabman that he was a detective named Sherlock Holmes, implying that he knows a lot about Sir Henry's movements in London (p. 74). 11. There is an escaped convict hiding in Devonshire (p. 84). 12. Mr. and Mrs. Barrymore; They will no longer be working for the Baskervilles now that Sir Charles is dead (pp. 86–88). 13. a woman sobbing somewhere in the house (p. 90)

Chapters 7–9, pp. 92–144: 1. When Watson asks Barrymore about the sobbing woman, his "pallid features…turned a shade paler" and Watson observes Mrs. Barrymore's red and swollen eyes (p. 93). 2. The boy who delivered the telegram gave it to Mrs. Barrymore, who claimed that her husband was upstairs and unavailable (pp. 94–95). 3. Jack Stapleton, a naturalist; He tells Watson that the peasants claim to have seen the legendary Hound of the Baskervilles (pp. 96–97). 4. He calls Watson by his name and inquires about Sherlock Holmes; Stapleton says that Dr. Mortimer told of Watson's arrival and that everyone knows he works for the great detective Sherlock Holmes (p. 98). 5. a great plain with hills sticking out of it, a swamp bog where ponies often get caught and die; claims to be able to cross it without getting caught in it (pp. 100–101) 6. Stapleton's sister, Miss Stapleton; she warns him to leave Baskerville Hall immediately; she thinks that Watson is Sir Henry (pp. 103–105) 7. In Watson's first report, he describes the moors. He tells of the convict who has not been seen since his escape, the strange Stapletons, and Sir Henry's interest in Miss Stapleton. He also relates the negative reaction of Stapleton to Sir Henry's interest in his sister. Watson describes a visit from Dr. Mortimer and the personality of Mr. Frankland of Lafter Hall. He concludes his report by telling Holmes of the Barrymores' suspicious actions—Mrs. Barrymore's emotional state and Mr. Barrymore's furtive movements at night (pp. 111–120). 8. In Watson's second report, he tells of the renovations being made to Baskerville Hall. He relates the story of his following Sir Henry and Miss Stapleton, only to have Stapleton interrupt the rendezvous and angrily accuse Sir Henry of several indiscretions. Watson tells of his and Sir Henry's plan to catch Barrymore sneaking around at night. They discover that Barrymore has been signaling to and feeding the criminal on the moor. His name is Selden, and he is Mrs. Barrymore's brother. Watson also tells Holmes how he and Sir Henry attempt to apprehend Selden. They hear the cry of the hound and see a dark figure on the moor (pp. 121–144). 9. He is grateful that Holmes trusts him to keep Sir Henry safe, but he is increasingly baffled by the events in and around Baskerville Hall. He ultimately wishes for Holmes to join him in Devonshire.

Chapters 10–12, pp. 145–193: 1. The weather remains gloomy, he continues to think of the hound's cries upon the moor, and he is puzzled by the stranger on the moor (pp. 145–147). 2. Barrymore has learned that Sir Henry and Watson have been looking for Selden (p. 148). 3. Sir Charles received a letter from a woman with the initials L.L., asking him to meet her at the gate by the moor. Barrymore did not reveal the information for fear of ruining the reputations of Sir Charles or the woman (pp. 150–151). 4. Dr. Mortimer tells him that L.L. is probably Laura Lyons, Frankland's daughter. She married a man who left her, and she has received monetary aid from several people, including Sir Charles and Stapleton (pp. 154–155). 5. He lives in one of the stone huts on the hillside, and a young boy brings him food and drink (p. 157). 6. beautiful and admirable, but with coarse facial expressions (pp. 160–161) 7. After her husband left her, she wanted to get a divorce, so she wrote to Sir Charles for help. She thought that if she could meet with Sir Charles and tell him her story, he would give her money for the divorce (pp. 162–165). 8. the exact location of the stranger on the moor; He has watched through his telescope to see the young boy bringing food to the stranger (pp. 170–171). 9. Sherlock Holmes (pp. 176–177) 10. He thought the investigation would be compromised if anyone knew he was there (p. 180). 11. Miss Stapleton is actually Stapleton's wife. Stapleton has promised to marry Laura Lyons upon her getting a divorce from her husband (pp. 181–183). 12. Stapleton owns the beastly hound and wishes to murder Sir Henry (p. 184). 13. He has been killed by the hound while crossing the moor. Barrymore gave him some of Sir Henry's clothes to wear, and the hound mistook him for Sir Henry (pp. 184–187). 14. Stapleton; He is very surprised but hides it quickly (pp. 190–191).

Chapters 13–15, pp. 194–240: 1. Stapleton is a Baskerville (p. 201). 2. He tells him that he and Watson are returning to London. He tells Sir Henry to keep his dinner appointment with the Stapletons and to walk home across the moors (pp. 202–204). 3. a London policeman named Lestrade (p. 205) 4. They need to tell her that Miss Stapleton is really Stapleton's wife, not his sister.

They also hope to get more information from her about Sir Charles' death (p. 206). 5. She explains that Stapleton told her to write the letter asking Sir Charles to meet her and then told her not to keep the appointment (pp. 207–208). 6. Stapleton and Sir Henry are sitting at the table inside the house. Miss Stapleton is nowhere to be seen (pp. 212–213). 7. He is chased and attacked by a huge, ferocious hound (pp. 216–217). 8. enormous, coal-black dog with fire spewing from its mouth; eyes glowing and its body outlined in flickering flames (p. 216) 9. It was covered with a phosphorous solution (p. 218). 10. Mrs. Stapleton; She reveals the abuse she suffered at her husband's hands and tells them where to find him (pp. 219–221). 11. Sir Henry's missing boot; Stapleton used it to give the hound Sir Henry's scent (p. 223). 12. He is lost in the Grimpen Mire while running from Holmes and Watson (p. 223). 13. He was Sir Charles' nephew, the son of the disinherited Rodger Baskerville. 14. He wanted to claim the Baskerville estate as his own. Everyone in the Baskerville family, as well as in Devonshire, knew and was afraid of the Hound of the Baskervilles (Chapter 15).

Note: Answers to Activities #8–#20 will vary. Suggested answers are given where applicable.

Activity #8: Sir Henry: bewildered, fearless, determined, stubborn; Miss Stapleton: beautiful, mysterious, manipulated, frightened; Sir Henry to Miss Stapleton: infatuated with her; Miss Stapleton to Sir Henry: worried about his safety

Activity #9: Title—*The Hound of the Baskervilles*; Setting—London, Baskerville Hall, and the Devonshire moors; Characters—Sherlock Holmes, Dr. Watson, Dr. Mortimer, Sir Henry Baskerville, the Barrymores, the Stapletons, Selden, and Laura Lyons; Problem—Sherlock Holmes must determine who or what is threatening Sir Henry Baskerville; Solution—Holmes devises a plan to reveal Stapleton as the murderer and owner of the hound; Series of Events—Sir Charles Baskerville dies; Dr. Mortimer comes to Sherlock Holmes for help in solving the mystery of his death; Sir Henry is threatened before he arrives at Baskerville Hall to claim the estate; Dr. Watson goes to Baskerville Hall to observe and report to Holmes; Watson meets the Stapletons and observes their strange relationship; It is discovered that Sir Charles was waiting to meet Laura Lyons before he died; A dark stranger is seen on the moor and discovered to be Sherlock Holmes; Selden, dressed like Sir Henry, is killed on the moor; Stapleton is revealed as the murderer.

Activity #10: p. 35, Sir Charles' cigar ashes had fallen twice, Sir Charles was waiting for someone; p. 93, Mrs. Barrymore is seen with red and swollen eyes, She is the woman Dr. Watson hears crying at night.

Activities #11–#12: Answers will vary.

Activity #13: Sir Charles: frightened, ailing, reclusive; Sir Henry: fearless, healthy, worldly; Both: Baskerville heirs, cursed by a giant hound, victims of Stapleton

Activities #14–#15: Answers will vary.

Activity #16: Sir Henry's missing boots; the Barrymores' decision to leave Baskerville Hall; Barrymore lying about his wife's crying; Laura Lyons' relationship with Sir Charles; Selden; Miss Stapleton; the dark stranger on the moor

Activity #17: Answers will vary.

Activity #18: Miss Stapleton: mysterious; beautiful, quiet woman who is obviously overpowered by her "brother"; used as a pawn by Stapleton to manipulate several people (i.e., Laura Lyons, Sir Henry); Answers will vary.

Activity #19: Causes—heir to the Baskerville estate; fear of the family curse; nightly walk on the moor; Laura Lyons' letter asking for help; ailing health; Stapleton's lies and manipulation

Activity #20: Answers will vary.

Quiz #1: 1. e 2. f 3. h 4. a 5. d 6. i 7. b 8. j 9. c 10. g

Quiz #2: A. 1. F 2. F 3. T 4. F 5. T 6. T **B.** 7. He is angry and refuses to be afraid. 8. visit 23 hotels to find the newspaper used for the note 9. He claims to be too busy with other cases to leave London. 10. The man told the cabman that he was a detective named Sherlock Holmes. 11. They plan to leave Baskerville Hall and start their own business with the money Sir Charles left to them. 12. He thinks they are gloomy, melancholy, and frightening.

Quiz #3: 1. Sir Henry 2. Baskerville Hall 3. Mrs. Barrymore 4. telegram 5. Stapleton 6. Grimpen Mire 7. howl 8. Hound of the Baskervilles 9. Miss Stapleton 10. Watson 11. Sir Henry 12. Baskerville Hall 13. Stapleton 14. Holmes 15. convict 16. Sir Henry 17. Barrymore 18. light or candle 19. Selden 20. brother 21. Mrs. Barrymore 22. food 23. Selden 24. dark stranger

Quiz #4: 1. c 2. b 3. a 4. c 5. b 6. c 7. d 8. b 9. d 10. a

Quiz #5: 1. j 2. f 3. g 4. h 5. i 6. d 7. e 8. a 9. b 10. c

Novel Test: A. 1. d 2. m 3. l 4. b 5. a 6. c 7. e 8. k 9. g 10. i 11. h 12. j 13. f **B.** 14. b 15. d 16. a 17. a 18. c 19. d 20. a 21. c 22. d 23. c 24. c 25. c 26. d 27. b 28. a 29. b 30. b **C.** 31. F 32. T 33. T 34. T 35. F 36. T 37. F 38. T **D.** Answers will vary. Refer to the scoring rubric on page 40 of this guide.

Activity #5:

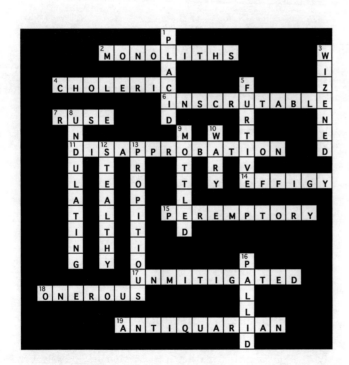

Linking Novel Units® Student Packets to National and State Reading Assessments

During the past several years, an increasing number of students have faced some form of state-mandated competency testing in reading. Many states now administer state-developed assessments to measure the skills and knowledge emphasized in their particular reading curriculum. This Novel Units® guide includes open-ended comprehension questions that correlate with state-mandated reading assessments. The rubric below provides important information for evaluating responses to open-ended comprehension questions. Teachers may also use scoring rubrics provided for their own state's competency test.

Scoring Rubric for Open-Ended Items

3-Exemplary
- Thorough, complete ideas/information
- Clear organization throughout
- Logical reasoning/conclusions
- Thorough understanding of reading task
- Accurate, complete response

2-Sufficient
- Many relevant ideas/pieces of information
- Clear organization throughout most of response
- Minor problems in logical reasoning/conclusions
- General understanding of reading task
- Generally accurate and complete response

1-Partially Sufficient
- Minimally relevant ideas/information
- Obvious gaps in organization
- Obvious problems in logical reasoning/conclusions
- Minimal understanding of reading task
- Inaccuracies/incomplete response

0-Insufficient
- Irrelevant ideas/information
- No coherent organization
- Major problems in logical reasoning/conclusions
- Little or no understanding of reading task
- Generally inaccurate/incomplete response